Lifelines 21

Joseph Paxton
An illustrated life of Sir Joseph Paxton
1803-1865
John Anthony

Shire Publications Ltd.

Joseph Paxton

Sir Joseph Paxton in the 1850s, from a contemporary photograph.

Contents

Chatsworth   5
Crystal Palaces   23
Sir Joseph   37
In the footsteps of Joseph Paxton   45
Bibliography   46
The principal events of Joseph Paxton's life   47
Index   48

ACKNOWLEDGEMENTS

The author wishes to thank the following for assistance in preparing this book: Paxton's great great grandchildren, Miss Persis Tallents and Mr. T. W. Tallents, who gave permission for their portraits of Paxton to be reproduced on page 2 and on the cover respectively; Mr. D. C. Bruce for help at Sydenham; Mr. T. S. Wragg for help at Chatsworth and Professor G. F. Chadwick. Quotations from the Paxton Papers and the diaries of the sixth Duke are included by permission of His Grace the Duke of Devonshire and the Trustees of the Chatsworth Settlement.

Illustrations on the pages indicated are acknowledged as follows: the Trustees of the Chatsworth Settlement 4, 13, 14, 15, 17; Edward Hubbard 10; Alan R. Warwick 21, 33 (bottom), 34, 35 (top and bottom), 42; Victoria and Albert Museum (Crown Copyright) 22 (top and bottom), 25, 26, 27, 28 (top and bottom), 29 (top and bottom), 31; Fox Photos 33 (top); National Monuments Record 39 (top and bottom), 41. The photographs on pages 9, 11 and 36 are by the author. The cover reproduces a water colour of Paxton in 1851, painted by Octavius Oakley; the cover design is by Robin Ollington.

Printed by Maund and Irvine Ltd., Tring, Herts.

Chatsworth

EARLY LIFE

Milton Bryan is a small village on the high lands of south Bedfordshire, very close to the Woburn estate of the Dukes of Bedford. Although now within a mile or two of the M1 motorway, the place is still quiet and entirely rural and it was here, in the depths of the English countryside, that Joseph Paxton was born on 3rd August 1803.

His mother appears to have made a runaway marriage with his father, William Paxton, but the latter died when Joseph, the seventh child, was still a boy. He was then sent to be brought up by an elder brother, but the arrangement does not seem to have been a happy one for Joseph ran away from home.

Somewhere about 1818 he seems to have had some kind of reconciliation with his family as he was working as a garden boy at Battlesden Park, within a mile of his birthplace. Several jobs then followed until, in 1823, he moved to the Horticultural Society at their newly established garden at Chiswick. Being but twenty years old he seems to have felt the need to appear older and he entered the date of his birth as 1801 not 1803. In this he seems to have deceived not only the Society but also posterity to some extent, for his date of birth is still occasionally given as 1801.

The garden of the Horticultural Society (now the Royal Horticultural Society) adjoined those of Chiswick House, then one of the smaller of the numerous residences of the Dukes of Devonshire. The sixth Duke, although not then particularly interested in horticulture, was in the habit of passing through a gate and strolling in the gardens of the Society. From time to time he came across a short, intelligent young man who was in charge of a section of the gardens. They had several

(Opposite) Joseph Paxton in 1836, a painting by Henry Perronet Briggs, R.A.

conversations and the Duke was impressed by the young man's abilities to such an extent that when a new head gardener was required at his great Derbyshire mansion of Chatsworth, Paxton was offered the job.

In later years it was said that Paxton had been contemplating emigration to the United States, but all this was put aside at his staggering stroke of good fortune. At twenty-three years of age he was to be in charge of the gardens of one of the greatest houses in the land. The Duke may well have acted upon impulse to some extent as he was about to depart for Russia as representative of George IV at the coronation of Tsar Nicholas I. At all events Paxton grasped the chance with both hands. Many years later he left the following account of his arrival at Chatsworth:

'I left London by the Comet Coach for Chesterfield; arrived at Chatsworth at 4.30 a.m. in the morning of the ninth of May 1826. As no person was to be seen at that early hour, I got over the greenhouse gate by the old covered way, explored the pleasure grounds and looked round the outside of the house. I then went down to the kitchen gardens, scaled the outside wall and saw the whole of the place, set the men to work there at six o'clock; then returned to Chatsworth and got Thomas Weldon to play me the water works and afterwards went to breakfast with poor dear Mrs Gregory and her niece. The latter fell in love with me and I with her, and thus completed my first morning's work at Chatsworth before nine o'clock'.

Two days later the Duke sailed for Russia.

WIFE AND DUKE

The housekeeper's niece was Miss Sarah Bown, a member of a family named Gregory long settled in the Matlock area. When she married Paxton in January 1827, nine months after their first meeting, she was twenty-six and he twenty-three. Her father was a substantial farmer, so substantial as to provide her with a dowry of £5,000. The new head gardener cannot have been regarded as any great match, for his salary was only £70 per year, but he at once began to discharge his duties with a degree of efficiency then quite novel for Chatsworth.

Sarah Paxton was to have an immense influence on the career of her husband. She had a strong personality but had the sense to subjugate this into support and not conflict with that of Paxton. She was the dominating influence on her family but by no means content with a world made up only of their needs and aspirations. Whilst his flair was essentially creative her contribution was that of management. He consulted her on all his affairs and the letters they wrote to each other during their frequent separations, now preserved at Chatsworth, reveal a woman reserved in nature and intensely involved in the career of her husband.

The other great influence upon Paxton's life was his master, William Spenser Cavendish, sixth Duke of Devonshire. Born in Paris in 1790, the son of Duchess Georgiana, one of the great beauties of her age, he never married but counted among his friends Dickens, Thackeray and Leigh Hunt. A man of wide culture, he travelled extensively and made important additions to his many houses and their contents. His naturally solitary disposition was reinforced by deafness and he took little part in public life. When in 1835 he declined appointment as Lord Chamberlain or as Lord Lieutenant of Ireland Lady Grenville wrote to him reproachfully of 'you and your Paxton sitting under a red rhododendron at Chatsworth, under the shade of palms and pines in your magnificent conservatory, and no thought of your country's weal and woe'.

HEAD GARDENER

At the time of Paxton's arrival at Chatsworth the Duke was in the midst of vast alterations to the great house, until then largely as it had been left in the early years of the eighteenth century. His architect was Jeffrey Wyattville and the works included the entirely new north wing. When Paxton appeared on the scene in 1826 much of the main constructional work was complete and internal decorations were under way.

Paxton set to work to organise his gardeners more effectively and to supervise everything they did with that efficiency which was later to become the hallmark of all his varied activities. Immediately the results were apparent. Then there were all the new works on the gardens,made necessary by the new buildings. In 1829, only three years after his arrival, he became head forester as well and began a long process of putting the estate woodlands into order after a long period of neglect. Almost at once he began planting the pinetum, a comprehensive collection of pines, many of them only recently introduced to this country.

With the resources of a great estate, Paxton was now able to give full rein to his inquiring mind by carrying out all sorts of horticultural experiments. He was especially interested in the problems of moving large trees, although means of doing this had been known much earlier. In 1830 he moved a large weeping ash from Derby to Chatsworth to form the centrepiece to the new north forecourt. Local opinion was doubtful of the widsom of trying to move so large a tree twenty-six miles but the tree survived and indeed flourishes still. 'Miraculous to have come so far', commented the Duke in his diary; 'I was enchanted with it.'

Ten years later he moved some palm trees from Walton-on-Thames to Chatsworth. The largest weighed twelve tons and eleven horses were needed to draw the special wagon. The palm house at Walton had to be demolished to get the trees out and turnpike gates had to be moved during the journey, but once more all went well.

His interests in botany are well demonstrated by his work on the pinetum; then, in 1835, he commenced the arboretum, a more comprehensive collection of trees of all kinds. In 1842 he began the rockworks set on the hillside with waterfalls over the Robbers Stone and the perpendicular cascade of the Wellington Rock. He built a broken aqueduct, from the end of which water falls to the tumbled rocks far below. Contemporaries marvelled at the skill with which these romantically simulated works of nature were designed. Now, with over a century of weathering and growth of vegetation, it seems incredible that they are works of man.

The enlargement of the great house made it desirable to move part of the village of Edensor, the western end of which intruded into the views of the park as seen from the house. Between 1838 and 1842 new cottages were built as replacements in some of the other ducal villages, but most of the new building was done by extending the village up a ravine to the east. Paxton seems to have had general responsibility for this work and, though assisted by John Robertson from 1840, he designed many of the new houses himself as well as the layout of the village. The style of the new building is derived from the picturesque tradition of the previous century with the addition of an astonishing variety of exotic designs. There are Swiss, Italian, Elizabethan and even Norman cottages and several that defy classification. The layout is in a carefully contrived picturesque manner, again reminiscent of the ideas of

8

Edensor, the estate village in Chatsworth Park designed by Paxton from 1845 to 1847.

the previous century in its studied lack of formality.

During these years Paxton was responsible for much other building on the estate, including his own house, Barbrook. This was a rebuilding, about 1843, of the cottage in the kitchen gardens which had earlier been the Paxtons' home. Robertson seems to have assisted in designing this new and more comfortable house to which a glass conservatory was attached. Here too Paxton had his offices from which his rapidly growing private practice was conducted.

PUBLIC PARKS

From quite an early period in Paxton's time at Chatsworth he appears to have had an understanding with the Duke that he might undertake work on his own account quite unconnected with that of his employer. As time passed this understanding extended to assistants in the estate office helping Paxton in his

9

Barbrook, Paxton's home at Chatsworth, photographed shortly before demolition a few years ago.

private projects. Young men who commenced their careers in the Chatsworth gardens appear later in charge of some of his outside projects. The accounts of Paxton's private practice have not survived and the detailed arrangements will now probably never be known, but it was probably more a matter of implicit understandings than any formal arrangement.

Prior to 1850 most of these private projects comprised the layout of public parks. The urban public park was then a new phenomenon in the industrial cities and it is not surprising that, as Paxton became increasingly well known in his profession, he should be asked to undertake such work.

The first commission came from Richard Yates in 1842 for Prince's Park, Liverpool. Ninety acres had been bought, of which fifty acres in the centre were to form the park, the surrounding land being for houses, either singly or in terraces. These houses would have the advantage of the pleasant parkland setting and be of such enhanced value as to cover the cost of laying out the park. This idea had already been used for Regent's Park, London, but at Liverpool sales of the houses were rather slow and most of the intended terraces were replaced by single houses. Within the park the main feature is a

The lake and ornamental planting in the south-eastern part of Prince's Park, Liverpool. The surrounding houses were built to finance the park layout.

naturalistic lake with islands surrounded by areas small in scale. This serves as a contrast to the broad expanses of grass in other parts. Around are belts of fine trees with an encircling drive, beyond which the surrounding houses can be glimpsed.

Paxton's outstanding achievement in this field is Birkenhead Park. This was the first park to be publicly promoted, being sponsored by the Improvement Commissioners who were building this, then new, town. Work began in 1844 and again a larger area was purchased than actually required for the park so that the extra land could be sold at values enhanced by the park. Numerous villas were built around the edges of the park itself. Paxton designed his two lakes so that the excavated earth could be used to create mounds to add visual interest to the even slope of the site. These mounds carry trees with shrubberies and sinuously winding paths between and are particularly attractive.

GLASSHOUSES

By 1828 Paxton had begun the long series of experiments in the design of glasshouses which was to culminate in the greatest glasshouse ever built and make the name of its builder a household word. General practice had been for such structures to have heavy frameworks with numerous ornamental embellishments. The result was expensive and also dark, and therefore unfavourable to plants. Paxton set his mind to devise cheaper, lighter structures.

Cast iron was then being introduced as a reasonably practical, if still novel, building material. Paxton appears to have carried out some experiments with this material, but then turned to wood and his writings contain many references to the superiority of wood over metal as being not only cheaper but also longer lasting, provided it is kept well painted.

He found that deflection of the rays of the sun would be minimised, and the heating effect of the sun therefore increased, if the sheets of glass were as nearly at right angles to the rays of the sun as possible. This could be done by having a ridge and furrow system instead of flat areas of glass and throughout his glass buildings Paxton adhered to this arrangement.

A further refinement, typical of its author, was a wooden glazing bar which had a channel for rain water on the outside and channels to catch condensation beneath each pane of glass on the inside. This glazing bar became so much associated with his name that it was called the 'Paxton gutter'.

These experiments produced a series of glasshouses in the Chatsworth kitchen gardens, a series which reached its culmination in the Great Conservatory. This vast structure was begun in 1836 and was completed and planted by 1840. It was very much the largest conservatory in the world, 277 feet long, 123 feet broad with a double curving roof rising to 67 feet in height. A carriage and pair could be driven through and there was an upper gallery from which one could look down upon the exotic plants. The heating system was served by a concealed roadway for fuel supplies and the boiler flue was carried up the hillside to a chimney stack concealed in the woods. The main structure was largely of wood, iron being used only for supporting columns.

The Great Conservatory caused a sensation, but it proved costly in maintenance. Apart from the cost of heating, the wooden members required constant painting, both inside and

(Opposite) An interior view of the Great Conservatory (1836–1839) with the carriage drive amidst the towering palms.

The Great Conservatory, photographed shortly before its demolition after the First World War, was 277ft long, 123ft broad and 67ft high.

out. During the First World War difficulties of labour and fuel supply led to the loss of many of the plants. Shortly after the war it was decided to demolish the Great Conservatory but this did not prove at all easy. By a strange irony it was Paxton's grandson, an engineer, who devised the means eventually used to demolish it.

VICTORIA REGIA

In 1846 seeds of a giant water-lily *Victoria regia* (now known as *Victoria amazonica*), which had been discovered on the Amazon in 1836, were sent to Kew. The plant grew but refused to flower. In 1849 Paxton obtained a plant from his friend Sir William Hooker, the Director at Kew. The plant had five leaves, the largest 5½ inches across.

At Chatsworth Paxton devised a tank to simulate as far as possible conditions on the Amazon. Heating and lighting were arranged and a water-wheel kept the water gently agitated. By mid September the leaves were 3½ feet in diameter. The tank was enlarged but still the plant grew. Bulletins on her progress were sent to the Duke in Ireland. By 15th October the leaf measured 4½ feet. On 2nd November a great bud appeared and by the 9th the plant was in full flower with a succession of buds. The Duke hurried from Ireland and the glasshouse was thronged with those who came to see the wonder. Paxton went to Windsor to present the Queen with a bud and a leaf. Paxton's youngest daughter Annie, aged seven, was put on one of the leaves and easily supported.

The success of *Victoria regia* created problems. A still larger tank was needed and Paxton devised a quite new type of building with a tank 33 feet in diameter. The roof was on the ridge and furrow principle and was supported by iron columns which were hollow and also used as drain pipes. Rain water was brought to these by the channels in the sash bars of Paxton's favourite design. The floor was of boarding with gaps between each board so that air could enter the building for ventilation and dust could be swept through.

Thus the new Lily House was a summary and refinement of all Paxton's years of experimenting with glasshouse design. The building was composed of standardised units which could be

The Lily House, built by Paxton to house Victoria regia, *the giant water-lily from the Amazon. Note Paxton's favourite ridge and furrow roofing system.*

used on a much larger scale. It was light, economical and simple. It was also the last major contribution Paxton was to make to Chatsworth.

SERVANT AND FRIEND

By 1840 Paxton had become the trusted confidant of the Duke, his duties of wide but ill-defined scope. His position was one which might have inspired all kinds of jealousies for, from being but one of a group of senior estate officials, he had become the real authority on all matters concerned with the estate. Even the Duke's lawyer, Benjamin Currey, found that Paxton was an essential channel in his dealings with the Duke.

Gradually a real friendship and close personal understanding developed between these two men of such contrasting backgrounds. In a letter to Paxton the Duke once wrote: 'I had rather all the flowers in the garden were dead than you ill.'

As early as 1834 Paxton accompanied the Duke on the first of several tours abroad. This one was to Paris where they bought plants and seeds, an indication of how far Paxton had succeeded in stimulating his master's interest in horticulture. Together they saw all the sights, including Versailles, where Paxton was rather disappointed with the fountains. He wrote home to Sarah: 'Well my love, the great day of the water works at Versailles came off yesterday, and a grand affair it was, not so much with the water works, which with two or three exceptions were not half so fine as I anticipated, but the fine Palace, the thousands and thousands of the "ton" of Paris gave it altogether an appearance beyond description.'

Tours to gardens in England followed, with the inevitable comparisons with Chatsworth. Then, in 1838, came a call from the Duke to join him in Switzerland for an extended tour on the Continent. The tour was occasioned by the Duke's emotional distress at the ending of the period of ten years during which he had lived with Elizabeth Warwick. The parting had been distressing and he turned for solace to the invaluable Paxton. They took a leisurely tour through Italy, then on to Athens and Constantinople. They were away for seven months and whilst this Grand Tour left an indelible impression upon him, Paxton felt keenly the prolonged separation from his growing family. In his absence Sarah coped with affairs at Chatsworth and their letters are full of concern for the estate. The birth of a daughter she dismisses in five lines.

The Emperor Fountain at Chatsworth, seen from the house. In the foreground is the Seahorse Fountain, a survivor of the formal gardens of the 1690s.

ROYAL OCCASIONS

In October 1832 Paxton's powers of organisation were given a new kind of test when Princess Victoria, then heir to the throne, visited Chatsworth with her mother, the Duchess of Kent. Among the festivities were fireworks and the fountains and Great Cascade were illuminated. Trees were planted to commemorate the event and in her diary, to which the future queen was already devoted, is recorded her surprise at the tidy appearance of the gardens each morning, no matter how great the crowds of people the previous evening. On inquiry she found that a hundred workmen had worked through the night sweeping the lawns and paths. Paxton, with his infinite capacity for taking pains, was at work.

In December 1843 a visit by Queen Victoria and Prince Albert again set Paxton the task of preparation for a royal occasion. He devised a vast scheme of illuminations with blue, crimson and green lights reflected in the pools in the gardens as the guests stood in the drawing-room. The Duke of Wellington came with the royal party and was much impressed. The next morning he got up early and was surprised by the overnight tidying-up which Paxton had repeated from the earlier visit. Later Wellington remarked to his host: 'I should have liked that man of yours for one of my generals.'

The following year another royal visit of a different kind loomed in prospect. The Duke was a personal friend of Tsar Nicholas I and when it was announced that he was to make a visit to this country it was naturally assumed that he would come to Chatsworth. Paxton suggested that a great fountain, work on which had already been commenced, should be completed in time for the visit. Over 100,000 cubic feet of earth were moved to make a reservoir on the moors above the house and work was pressed ahead. The Tsar arrived sooner than expected but was unable to spare time to come to Chatsworth and thus never saw the fountain named in his honour the Emperor Fountain. Today the great fountain remains perhaps the most impressive of Paxton's works to be seen at Chatsworth, still able to throw its waters to a height of 290 feet above the gardens.

PAXTON AS WRITER

In 1831 there occurred the rather surprising development of the head gardener taking to journalism. He started a monthly magazine called the *Horticultural Register* and three years later this was accompanied by a more elaborate periodical, the *Magazine of Botany and Register of Flowering Plants* with fine coloured plates. That Paxton, with his meagre formal education, could edit successful magazines of this nature shows that the fluent pen of a journalist can be developed far from the schoolroom. The money for these publishing ventures may well have come from his wife and indeed that formidable lady may have contributed more than money to the inevitably complex and challenging work of periodical publishing.

Although Paxton gave up the editorship of the *Horticultural Register* in 1835 he wrote extensively in this middle period of his life. In 1838 *A Practical Treatise on the Cultivation of the Dahlia* caused something of a sensation, being translated into several European languages. The *Pocket Botanical Dictionary* followed in 1840 in which he collaborated with Dr Lindley. Ten years later the same pair issued *Paxton's Flower Garden* and Paxton alone was responsible for the *Calendar of Garden Operations* about the same time. The latter was popular for the better part of a century in its various revised forms.

Paxton ceased his *Magazine of Botany* in 1849, but in 1841 had founded a new weekly paper, the *Gardeners Chronicle,* with Dr Lindley. Such was the success of this venture that the paper is still flourishing today.

In 1845 Paxton was one of four partners who launched the *Daily News* as a new national daily paper, Paxton subscribing £25,000, the largest share. The *Daily News* had an unhappy start, even though no less a figure than Charles Dickens had been engaged as editor. The great novelist proved quite unsuited to the task and only lasted three weeks and it is difficult to believe that Paxton was at all equipped for the highly specialised task of launching a national newspaper. After a short time he seems to have withdrawn from active involvement in the paper.

RAILWAYS

During the 1840s the country was fascinated by the new railways and it was natural that Paxton, with his innovating mind, should have become involved. To some extent this was a consequence of his work for the Duke, as the latter owned land all over the country which was inevitably invaded by the developing railway network. But Paxton's involvement went far beyond this. From the effective start of railways in 1830 he had been excited by the prospects of the new inventions. He was on terms of friendship with many of the leading figures in the railway world, with the Stephensons, father and son, with Thomas Brassey the contractor and with George Wythes.

Speculation in railways became increasingly hectic during the early forties and both Paxton and his wife were heavily involved. If anything Sarah displayed the cooler judgement and when the inevitable crash came in 1845 the Paxtons remained unscathed.

In 1848 Paxton became a director of the Midland Railway. This brought him into contact with George Hudson, famous as the 'Railway King'. Ultimately discredited, Hudson was immensely successful at a time when big business was in its infancy and appreciated the value of a railway system as opposed to a mere collection of lines. Although Sarah never liked Hudson the contact was to prove valuable when the Duke got into serious financial trouble and Hudson purchased some estates.

On railway finance Paxton had views which were typical of the age. He believed that all forms of government supervision must be bad. Any notion that railways, as a public service, ought to be subject to public control was anathema to him.

The earlier years at Chatsworth seem to have been the happiest ones of Paxton's life. He had an absorbing job and a congenial master who allowed him the widest latitude to undertake outside work. He had a happy family life with additions appearing at frequent intervals, six daughters and one son. Frequent absences only served to emphasise the pleasures of return.

From the 1840s, however, his increasing outside interests built up to exert almost intolerable pressure. He was now away for long periods with constant travel in the uncomfortable trains of the period; indeed he led a life for the first time made possible by the new railways.

The account of a business tour late in 1845 well illustrates Paxton's formidable powers of work and the extraordinary extent to which Victorian men of business drove themselves. Writing to Sarah, who was always demanding and expecting letters from him on all he did when away from home, he says:

'I left you at Sheffield per mail, arrived safe in London and lay down for two hours; then got up and began business. Our meeting at the Isle of Wight lasted for two hours. I had from one to two to go and see Canon; at two we commenced upon the Southampton projects, which lasted until five. Without getting a morsel of food I started off again for Derby, and from eight in the morning until we arrived at Wolverton, I had not touched food or drunk even a glass of water. I got to Derby about half past eleven (p.m.), where I found the Sheffield deputation waiting for me. We sat discussing matters over until three in the morning; I had to be at breakfast by seven o'clock to be ready to start with the Midland directors to Gloucester and Bristol. After a hard day at Birmingham and Cheltenham and Gloucester we got to dinner at Bristol about eight o'clock. We had a very large party, and did not break up until two o'clock in the morning. The next morning was engaged in seeing the corporation of Bristol and other things. About this time Mr Hudson expressed his wish to purchase all the Londesborough property, and it was agreed I should start by the half past five o'clock train to London to see Mr Curry. After we had finished Bristol, Mrs Hudson, who had come down in the train, wanted

A meeting of railway directors in the 1850s or 60s. Paxton is seated on the extreme left. The man seated to the left of the central standing figure is Charles Fox (later knighted) of Fox and Henderson, contractors for the Crystal Palace.

Mr Hudson to take her to Bath, and got there just in time to see a few of the sights before dark. I got up next morning at a quarter before five and went along to London to see Mr Curry. After a good deal of bother I found out that he was at Eltham in Kent, nine miles from London. I therefore took a cab and called up Bradbury, who went with me, and on my return I called at Canon's and got Bradbury to write you a few lines while I did business with Canon. I then started with Tootal and Wheeler to Birmingham; got there at half past twelve and got a deputation of railway people out of bed at one o'clock; sat till three; went to bed and started off at six o'clock this morning to Derby and came on to York.'

In view of such a mode of life it is hardly surprising that his letters home constantly complain of ill health. Sarah urged him to cut down his activities and to leave more to others, appeals which were echoed by his doctor. But Paxton had become almost obsessed by the fascination of doing business — it hardly mattered what business. His endless activities began to exert a serious strain on his by no means hardy constitution. Eventually the body called a halt that would not be denied, but for the time being he met the warning signs by taking on yet more work, indeed he was about to embark upon the greatest enterprise of his life.

21

(Above) The official painting of the Royal Commissioners for the Exhibition of 1851, by H. W. Philips. Prince Albert sits examining plans, Paxton leans forward with his hand on the table. In the centre foreground sits William Cubitt, the architect, and behind him stands Charles Fox.

(Below) The design for the exhibition building prepared by the building committee, as published in Illustrated London News, *22nd January 1850.*

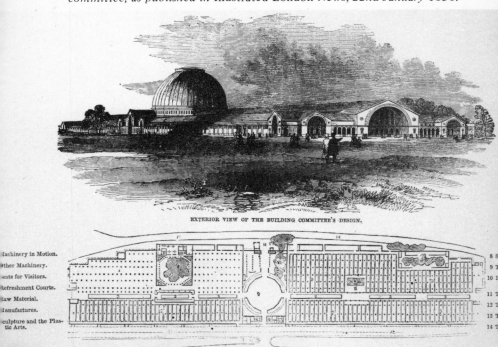

EXTERIOR VIEW OF THE BUILDING COMMITTEE'S DESIGN.

Machinery in Motion.
ther Machinery.
eats for Visitors.
Refreshment Courts.
Raw Material.
Manufactures.
culpture and the Plas-
tic Arts.

8 Sm
9 Th
10 Pr
E.
11 Th
12 Th
13 Th
14 Th
B

GROUND PLAN OF THE BUILDING COMMITTEE'S DESIGN.

Crystal Palaces

THE GREAT EXHIBITION

The 'Great Exhibition of the Works of All Nations' was conceived at the Royal Society of Arts. Prince Albert had become President in 1845 and the idea for the mammoth exhibition seems to have germinated between the Prince and Henry Cole, a civil servant and leading member of the Society. The exhibition was an attempt to raise the standard of design of manufactured articles of all kinds. Such exhibitions had been held before, but never on this scale or with international scope. Under the leadership of the Prince the project went ahead and at length a site on the south side of Hyde Park was agreed upon, a condition being that the building for the exhibition be subsequently removed.

In January 1850 a Royal Commission was appointed to undertake the exhibition, financed not by the Government but by private subscriptions and guarantees for loans from the Bank of England. A building committee was set up and arranged an international competition for the design of the building. In April 245 designs were received, among them several for iron and glass structures. But the committee regarded all the designs as being either too expensive or impossible to build in the time available. They produced a scheme of their own, a largely brick structure with a dome two hundred feet in diameter. This was even more expensive and impractical than most of the competition entries and apart from these defects it was also very ugly. There was a public outcry against both building and exhibition of such dimensions that the whole enterprise seemed about to end in fiasco.

The controversy was at its height when Paxton, on 11th July 1850, went to see Mr Ellis, chairman of the Midland Railway, at the newly built chamber of the House of Commons. Tests were being made on the acoustics, which turned out to be very poor. Paxton remarked that he feared that another mistake would be made over the exhibition building and that he had had one or two ideas of his own. Mr Ellis urged him to put his ideas forward even though the specification was to be issued in a fortnight. At the Board of Trade office Mr Cole told them that the design was already settled but that the specification might contain a clause that tenderers might submit a price for a design of their own as well as for the official design. Paxton then offered to have a design and a price ready in nine days time if such a clause were included.

Paxton next went to Hyde Park to see the site but could do nothing over the ensuing weekend as he had agreed to go to North Wales to see the floating into position of the third tube of the Britannia Bridge across the Menai Straits. By Tuesday he was at Derby as chairman of the Works and Ways Committee of the Midland Railway. The business included trying a pointsman for some minor offence. It was noticed that the chairman made copious notes on a large sheet of blotting paper. As he had made so many notes it was agreed to take the decision from him and they let the offending pointsman off with a 5s fine. Then holding up the blotting paper Paxton said: 'This is a design for the Great Industrial Exhibition to be held in Hyde Park.'

The sheet of blotting paper is now among the treasures of the Victoria and Albert Museum, for all the essential features of the Crystal Palace were shown. It was a cross section and end elevation of a building based upon the Lily House at Chatsworth, although on a vastly larger scale. Paxton took his sketch to his office at Chatsworth where his assistants worked through several days and nights feverishly preparing detailed plans. William Barlow, engineer to the Midland Railway, was called in to check the soundness of the structure.

On 21st June Paxton set out with his plans for London. On Derby station he chanced to meet Robert Stephenson who was travelling on the same train. Stephenson was one of the royal commissioners and one of the leading civil engineers of the day. To Paxton's remarks about his plans he pointed out that all was now settled but he agreed to look them over whilst Paxton ate his packed dinner (this was before the days of restaurant cars). Stephenson lit a cigar, which Paxton noticed went out without

(Opposite) The blotting paper sketch made by Paxton at Derby on 11th June 1850 showing the essential features of his exhibition building. Top is a section and below an end elevation. Below the sketches is the telegram to Sarah Paxton informing her of the acceptance of the design.

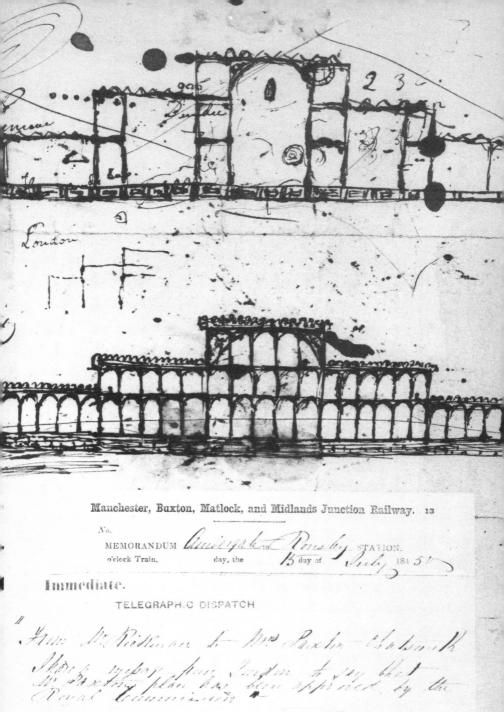

Manchester, Buxton, Matlock, and Midlands Junction Railway. 13

No.

MEMORANDUM *Cromford and Rowsley* STATION.

o'clock Train. day, the *15* day of *July* 184 *5*

Immediate.

TELEGRAPHIC DISPATCH

From Mr Rickman to Mr Paxton Chatsworth I hereby express from London to say that Mr Paxtons plan has been approved by the Royal Commission the smoker seeming to be aware of the fact. At length he rolled up the plans, saying 'admirable', and although he thought it too late he agreed to place the plans before the Royal Commission.

Paxton had a long interview with Prince Albert on 24th June and the Prince was impressed. The commission saw the design on the 22nd and again considered it on the 29th, but although there was much support for Paxton's design the majority feeling was that the question of the design had already been settled.

Then Paxton decided to appeal directly to the public. He had

The glazing wagon which ran on wheels in the gutter of Paxton's patent roofing system and which enabled four men to work at once. The wagon could be covered in wet weather.

a drawing of his design published in the *Illustrated London News*. Public reaction was enthusiastic. In the face of this the building committee informed Paxton that if he sent in a tender for his design it would be considered.

Paxton had already been in touch with Messrs Fox and Henderson, who were primarily railway equipment manufacturers, and had contacted possible makers of the iron components and the enormous quantities of glass required. Within a week working drawings and detailed estimates were prepared for submission to the commission on 10th July. On 15th July he telegraphed to Sarah at Chatsworth that his design

Testing the galleries of the Crystal Palace. A section was built on the ground and tested by marching troops.

had been approved unanimously by both the commission and the building committee.

There were now nine months to go before the exhibition was due to open and the speed with which the vast structure rose astonished the world. The secret lay in the design being based upon the repetition of standard components. Much of the work could be done away from the site and on arrival at Hyde Park the iron columns and girders were simply bolted together. No scaffolding was needed, only blocks and pulleys, masts, sheer legs and ropes. At one period three columns and two girders were being erected every sixteen minutes. The wooden sash bars for the enormous expanse of Paxton's now patented roofing system were cut on site by the machines he had developed at Chatsworth and seventy-six trolleys running along the gutters each enabled two glaziers to fix the glass sheets in place, sheets larger than any that had been made previously.

During the frantic consideration of the design by the building committee many modifications were made. The most important of these was the insertion of a transept across the centre of the building. This transept was given added prominence by the semicircular roof, constructed largely of wood, on the lines of that of the Great Conservatory, and

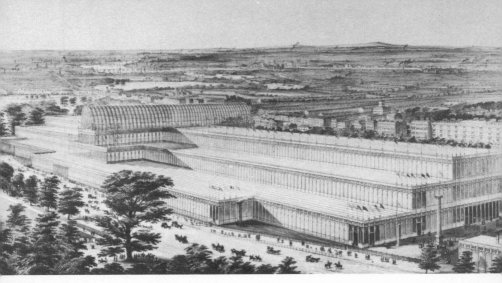

(Above) The Crystal Palace from the north-west with central London in the background – the 'aeronautic' view, finest of many pictures drawn and painted and lithographed in 1851. (Below) The opening ceremony, 1st May 1851. On the dais are the Queen and royal party. In the centre stands Ostler's crystal fountain. (A lithograph by Dickinson).

(Above) The north-west corner of the Crystal Palace. The flags are blurred due to the long time exposure needed for the calotype process. (Below) The eastern section of the nave looking towards the transept. A calotype photograph taken on a Sunday when the exhibition was closed. This part of the building housed the foreign exhibits.

enabling a number of elm trees to be preserved by having them inside the building.

As work progressed five hundred painters swarmed over the building, whilst inside unbleached calico was stretched between the roof ridges and over the south facade to control the glare of the sun. Thus a building 1,848 feet long by 408 feet wide, with a transept 72 feet wide and 108 feet high, was built in a little over six months.

Public and press alike were delighted with this light, almost fairy-like palace. It was in the pages of *Punch* that the name 'Crystal Palace' was coined.

But Paxton was unpopular in some professional circles. *The Builder* hinted at family influence, as the nephew of the Duke of Devonshire, Lord Granville, was chairman of the finance committee of the commission. Paxton fully acknowledged the help given by numerous professionals including I. K. Brunel, the engineer, and Charles Barry, the architect. Even so 233 competitors had seen their schemes turned down in favour of a gardener who had not even entered the competition. Yet there was no serious ill-will. Through life Paxton seems to have been able to rise to great achievements without becoming conceited or overbearing. The Crystal Palace made him the hero of the nation, yet he still behaved as he had as a simple gardener. As the exhibition closed in October 1851 he was knighted for his services.

THE SYDENHAM CRYSTAL PALACE

From the start Paxton had the permanent retention of the Crystal Palace in mind and he campaigned ardently to this end. His pamphlet 'What is to become of the Crystal Palace?' received much support. *The Times* and *Punch* were strongly in support. But Prince Albert thought it should go and, after much discussion and a Parliamentary committee on the matter, the House of Commons voted for its removal.

Paxton had prepared for this decision by setting in motion the formation of a public company to buy the building from Fox and Henderson for £70,000. The Crystal Palace never belonged to the Royal Commission who merely rented it with an option to purchase which was never exercised.

After inspecting a number of possible sites, the grounds of Penge Place, a large country house at Sydenham to the south-east of London, were bought. There were fine views to

PRAISE AND PUDDING.

H.R.H. Pr-nce Albert.—"Master Joseph Paxton—In Addition to the Honours that have been heaped upon You, I have much Pleasure in Presenting You with this Piece of 'Solid Pudding.'"

A cartoon in Punch, *25th October 1851. In fact Paxton received £5,000 from the profits made by the exhibition.*

the south and east over still rural Kent and Surrey, but the main advantage of the site was the possibility of providing rail access to London to bring the hoped-for millions of visitors. The Brighton Railway was financially interested in the Crystal Palace Company from the beginning and Samuel Laing was chairman of both.

Naturally Paxton was a director of the company, nominally as Director of the Winter Garden, Park and Conservatory, but in fact the moving spirit behind the whole enterprise. He redesigned his building on even more expansive lines with double the glass area of the Hyde Park building and half as much cubic capacity again. There were now three transepts instead of the original one and wrought iron took the place of much of the wood used in Hyde Park. Whilst undeniably impressive, if only by its immense size, the splendid simplicity of the earlier structure was lost.

The function of the new building was that of a palace of leisure instead of a palace of industry. The aim was to improve the minds of the millions. On either side of the nave and in the wings were courts equipped with plaster casts and other reproductions to evoke the civilisations of Rome, Egypt, Byzantium and even more remote ages. At the same time entertainment was to be provided as a magnet to draw the masses to this cornucopia of possibly somewhat second-hand culture. There was also the incidental intention that those concerned might make fortunes for themselves in the process.

In the early days the venture was surrounded by much optimism and capital was easily forthcoming. Gradually the optimism faded. Rebuilding took much longer than expected and costs rose. Sydenham was then in rural Kent and it took time for Londoners to become accustomed to travelling out to such a novelty. The main reason for the financial difficulties which constantly dogged the Sydenham Crystal Palace was undoubtedly the extravagances of the scheme itself. The building itself was extravagant, and even more so were the elaborate substructure and terracing needed as a base on the hilltop site. But the supreme extravagance was the design for the gardens. Here Paxton was determined to outdo Versailles and his enthusiasm carried all before him. The water works comprised fountains with almost twelve thousand jets, cascades, canals and lakes. Two water towers were needed at either end of the palace to provide the necessary head of water and 120,000

(Above) An air view
of the Sydenham
Crystal Palace said
to have been taken
from a balloon. The
north transept was
burned down in
1866 and never
replaced. Rockhills,
Paxton's home, can be
seen to the right of
the mid height of
the north tower in
the top centre of
the picture.

(Left) An interior
view of the nave
nearing completion
at Sydenham,
September 1853.
A photograph by
Delamotte.

The opening ceremony at Sydenham, 10th June 1854. Behind the royal party rises the choir of 1,500 singers who sang the Hallelujah Chorus with a band augmented with 200 brass instruments.

gallons per minute were needed when the whole was in full play.

The immense layout had an unmistakable Italianate air about it. The terraces below the palace were embellished with elaborate balustrades and statuary and there was a great central vista with cascades and formal pools either side. In other parts of the gardens there was informal, picturesque landscaping with winding walks among tree-clad mounds. On an island in one of the two lakes were displayed prehistoric monsters in replica, and they remain there today.

The general verdict on the Sydenham Crystal Palace was that it was a greater triumph even than Hyde Park. The concerts held

(Left) An interior view taken a few months before the fire of 1936. In the centre Ostler's crystal fountain still stands in the place of honour, as _it_ did in 1851.

(Below) The fire of 30th November 1936 which destroyed the Sydenham Crystal Palace.

there became especially famous and the Handel festivals held from 1857 were on a scale previously unknown in England. Later it was to be especially known for brass bands and firework displays.

Yet the question remains; how did Paxton, the man of business with an infinite capacity for taking pains, with his utter faith in the limited liability company, come to overspend so disastrously? Whilst many others were involved it was Paxton who held the main responsibility.

The cares of Sydenham came to Paxton at a time of steadily deteriorating health. In his letters he refers to troublesome meetings of the company and the discontented shareholders. He still held his posts at Chatsworth, although more and more Sarah was left to cope with affairs there, aided by sub-agents. The Duke's health was breaking up and he was constantly on the move between his many houses and often wanting the solace of Paxton. In addition he had a varied programme of other activities.

Sydenham involved Paxton in spending the greater part of his time there and he leased a house from the company, Rockhills, which adjoined the north end of the palace grounds. Here he entertained much, for he was always fond of good food and drink, a partiality which had an effect on his waistline as the years passed. Here the Duke often came, sometimes to stay for weeks, and here Paxton often had the company of his daughters, some now married and living nearby. But Sarah never liked Sydenham and in their letters deplored the rift with their old life at Chatsworth.

Some of the last remaining terraces of the once vast garden layout at Sydenham.

Sir Joseph

THE ARCHITECT

After 1850 the focal point of Paxton's activities tended to be London rather than Chatsworth and he had staff at Sydenham as well as at various offices in central London. From about this time also G. H. Stokes appears to have become his architectural assistant and in 1853 married his eldest daughter. As his father-in-law became increasingly preoccupied at Sydenham his participation in the architectural work of the firm increased, although Paxton always remained very much the principal.

The fame of the Crystal Palace stimulated many similar projects. In 1851 Paxton prepared a design for a Crystal Palace in New York and ten years later for one in Paris. 1851 also saw designs for roofing over the courtyard of the Royal Exchange in London using his roofing system and for a glass 'Sanitarium' for the London Chest Hospital. Nothing came of any of these proposals and after Sydenham he built nothing more in this idiom. This was undoubtedly a great disappointment for in 1851 many people besides Paxton believed that a great future awaited the iron and glass building. It was felt that all kinds of buildings could be built in this way ranging from hospitals to assembly halls. With the possible exception of the entirely new building type of the railway station, no such new dawn in architecture occurred.

The reason is doubtless that the Hyde Park Crystal Palace was quite outside the main stream of architectural thought of the nineteenth century. The trend was towards an eclectic revival of the styles of the past and the Crystal Palace was of no style at all. It might well be agreed that it was delightful and served its purpose admirably, but it was not architecture. To be architecture it was felt that a building must have solidity, and the Crystal Palace relied for its effect upon the very absence of this quality. The Sydenham Crystal Palace represents a significant move in the direction of greater solidity, with its massive base and elaborated central feature with subsidiary features symmetrically disposed either side.

Paxton himself, perhaps unconsciously, shared some of this feeling that a glass building cannot be architecture of a respectable kind. The Great Conservatory was sited in a clearing in a wood and could not be seen from the windows of Chatsworth. His extensive practice in conventional buildings always kept well within the accepted styles of the day.

By 1850 Paxton had already been commissioned to build Mentmore in Buckinghamshire for Baron Mayer Rothschild. The great house, surrounding park and estate village were all designed by Paxton and Stokes and work went on until 1859. The house would seem to have been modelled on the great Elizabethan mansion of Wollaton, near Nottingham, but with the substitution of a great hall lit by a glass roof for the towering feature above the central hall at Wollaton.

Paxton seems almost to have become architect to the Rothschild family for in 1853 he began work on a house for Baron James de Rothschild at Ferrières, near Paris. This is rather similar in form to Mentmore, although rather larger and in the Third Empire style of the time. The gardens are of course by Paxton and are quite extensive in comparison with the surprisingly modest layout at Mentmore. Other work for the great family of financiers was mainly carried out by Stokes and included two enlargements of the house at Aston Clinton, Buckinghamshire, now demolished, and a house at Pregny, near Geneva.

Paxton continued to design public parks, including Kelvingrove Park and Queen's Park, Glasgow, and the People's Park, Halifax. Extensions to the Spa buildings and grounds at Scarborough, where the Paxtons had long taken their summer holidays, followed in 1858.

The last large-scale building project brought Paxton back to Battlesden where he had worked as an under-gardener forty years before. In 1864 he and Stokes built a new house here, but it has long since been demolished.

A recurring feature of Paxton's architectural work is the attention given to the services such as heating and ventilation which often included novel features. In matters of style he was much less given to innovation and his work could easily pass for that of many other architects of the day. As time went on Stokes seems to have taken over more and more of the detailed

(Above) Part of the gardens laid out by Paxton at Mentmore, Buckinghamshire.

(Below) The south side of Mentmore with the conservatory on the right.

work and Paxton expected that he would continue the firm after his death. It is a commentary on their relationship that after Paxton's death Stokes ceased practice altogether as soon as he had completed work in hand.

Paxton was never trained as an architect but at a time when all architectural education was as a subordinate in an office this did not differentiate him so greatly from other architects. After 1850 he frequently signed drawings 'Joseph Paxton, Architect' and the extent and nature of his works suggests that he was well justified in doing so.

MEMBER OF PARLIAMENT

Paxton became one of the two members of Parliament for Coventry in December 1854. At that time it was considered a fitting mark of a successful career to take a Parliamentary seat but Paxton was never an effective speaker or debater. He was useful in committee where his good sense and experience came to be respected and he attended to the needs of his constituents rather more conscientiously than was usual at the time. Parliament, of course, meant yet more calls on his time. His health was deteriorating but he took no heed of the warning signs and increased the pace of his activities still further.

Paxton had first had connections with Coventry when he laid out a cemetery there in 1845. In 1854 the town was in an unhappy condition. Free trade had meant widespread unemployment in the traditional silk-ribbon industry. Social conditions were bad and industrial relations were worse. All this was new to Paxton. As the retainer of a great Whig house he was, of course, a Liberal. In the event, in spite of vociferous opposition, the Tories were unable to find a candidate and Paxton was returned unopposed.

He seems to have faced the rough and tumble of politics in a nineteenth-century industrial town with his usual good humour, but Sarah never wavered in her dislike of his parliamentary duties or of Coventry and its electors. She wrote of 'the scum of Coventry' and, wisely, refrained from canvassing for him.

His lifelong habit of independent thought is reflected in his being one of the sixteen Liberal members who revolted under Cobden to bring down the government of Palmerston in 1857, thus forcing a general election. The issue concerned the bombardment of Canton by the Royal Navy. He objected strongly to this high-handed action upon a defenceless city and

Coventry Cemetery, laid out by Paxton between 1845 and 1847. A memorial to Paxton can be seen on the left.

posterity has upheld his judgement. He retained his seat easily in the election and again in that of 1859.

Paxton was a convinced Free-Trader and the Commercial Treaty with France of 1860 brought embarrassments. One effect was to remove the duty on French silk and this caused dismay in Coventry where unemployment among the silk workers was already high. Paxton and Mr Ellice, the other member for the town, tried to obtain transitional arrangements to ease the blow, but Parliament passed the treaty as it stood. The ensuing slump was due to other causes as well as the treaty, but in 1862 thousands were out of work and relief funds failed to alleviate the distress. Paxton saw that other sources of employment were needed. Cotton, worsted and woollen mills were started and Paxton set men to work to clear a common.

Parliament also involved Paxton in the organisation of the Army Works Corps in the Crimea in 1854. This civilian force, largely recruited from the navvies at Sydenham, made some contribution to relieving the chaos before Sebastopol but relations with the military were never satisfactory and at times acrimonious.

Rockhills, the house at Sydenham leased by Paxton from the Crystal Palace Company, and where he died in 1865. The figure in the white top hat leaning on the garden urn is said to be Paxton. (A photograph of about 1860)

In 1855 he appeared before a Parliamentary Committee on Metropolitan Communications with a proposal for a Great Victorian Way. This was to be an immense boulevard of glass and iron eleven and a half miles long and incorporating a road and railway with commercial development. Characteristically he proposed that this should be carried out by a limited liability company. Around 1860 he was active in promoting the Thames Graving Dock; he gave evidence to a committee on the condition of the Serpentine in Hyde Park and he was chairman of the Select Committee of the House of Commons on the Thames Embankment. Later he promoted the act which authorised construction of the embankment incorporating a road, underground railway and trunk sewer.

LAST YEARS

Towards the end a change came over the relations between husband and wife. Two people had found fame and fortune but had lost happiness.

Sarah was a reserved and in some ways a difficult woman but her love for her husband and her devotion made his career possible. She rejoiced in his success, but this very success swept him from her. Whilst not jealous, she was certainly possessive. She failed to realise that London and Sydenham were different worlds to Chatsworth. He was happy in all three places but Sarah always looked upon the old home at Chatsworth as her anchor. Gradually their lives drifted apart. He cut a figure in society whilst she, until 1858, was his deputy at Chatsworth. Suffering from constant headaches, she worked late at night on estate papers, drinking cups of strong coffee to stay awake. Constantly she complained in her letters, and the complaints doubtless drove them further apart. 'You would not regret a visit to Chatsworth if only to see the Rhododendrons and the great beauty of the place', she writes. 'Our beautiful flowers will bloom and die and you will never see them.' 'I never saw Chatsworth look more lovely and you are not here.' 'O Fame, would that I could break your trumpet.' And often, 'I am very lonely.'

Paxton had all the excitement of doing business, but he too had lost the secret of contentment. The fascination of business affairs and making money drove him on but he had lost his peace of mind. The warning signs of his increasing ill-health were ignored.

In the midst of all his distractions Paxton greatly loved his children. Two of his elder daughters, when married, lived in London and were often at Rockhills. Sarah sent down hampers of dainties and often a haunch of venison, fruit and Derbyshire black puddings. But in one respect her conduct was particularly unfortunate. She never made his humble Bedfordshire relations welcome at Chatsworth although he always took care to keep in touch. He deeply resented this. Talking to one of his daughters on the eve of her marriage he said: 'Always, my dear, be kind to your husband's relations. Your mother has not been kind to mine.'

The memories of his humble origins lingered with him all his life. Once, when his fondness for a good table had long since left its mark on his waistline, he remarked suddenly: 'You never know how much nourishment there is in a turnip until you have had to live on it.'

He was careful in his clothes, being noted for his white top hat, and had a taste for fancy waistcoats. Sarah too was always interested in clothes and wanted details of the dresses worn at the parties he attended in London. He was often in Paris in these latter years and her present on his return would often be a gown.

On 18th January 1858 the sixth Duke of Devonshire died in his sleep at Hardwick. Although partly paralysed since a stroke in 1854 his death was sudden and found Paxton at Bolton Abbey, a Yorkshire residence of the Duke. He hurried to perform his final service for his friend and master in arranging the funeral with that efficiency and attention to detail which marked his other services. Condolences poured in upon Paxton as much as upon members of the family, for apart from his sisters the Duke had no near relatives and was succeeded by a distant cousin. Although many members of the Cavendish family followed the coffin through Edensor churchyard, the chief mourner was Paxton.

On 27th January Paxton wrote to the new Duke resigning all his offices at Chatsworth. In reply the Duke offered him the use of his house at Chatsworth for the rest of his days and in the event Paxton's services were retained as an adviser. He was frequently consulted and the following year an annual salary of £500 a year was paid him. The new Duke found the financial position of the estate far from satisfactory and a reduction in staff called for. Paxton was much concerned to find employment for the workers who had to be discharged. His visits to Derbyshire were irregular but when there he was treated with great honour by the seventh Duke and his family.

Sarah at last laid down her duties at Chatsworth. She was now often at London or Sydenham and even went abroad. Yet her heart remained at Chatsworth and here she spent the greater part of the year. She continued to keep a careful eye on the money market and continued to concern herself with property as Paxton by now owned a good deal in Derbyshire. After his death she lived on at Barbrook where the seventh Duke often called on her.

After 1858 Paxton, though in failing health, lived through busy years. He entertained much, Mr and Mrs Gladstone being frequent guests. He was wealthy and respected, even though the wilder excesses of praise of 1851 had by then been somewhat tempered.

He was invited to visit the United States on railway business by Cobden but pressure of other work prevented this. Ferrières occupied him a good deal in 1859 as did the Graving Dock and railways in 1859, and 1861 saw him in Spain on railway business.

Paxton disapproved of the International Exhibition of 1862 and took no part in it. It made a loss largely due to the expensive and ugly building erected for it. But there was no pause in the schemes with which he concerned himself in these last years, and at the age of fify-eight he even appeared before the world as a captain in the Matlock Rifles, but failing health forced him to retire from Parliament in the spring of 1865.

At the end of May that year there was a flower show in the Crystal Palace and Paxton was wheeled in a chair into his great building for the last time. Although surrounded by the plants he had always loved he was unable to complete the tour. He died at dawn on 8th June 1865.

IN THE FOOTSTEPS OF JOSEPH PAXTON

At Milton Bryan, Bedfordshire, there is a stained glass memorial window in the church and there are memorials at Coventry Cemetery and in the Crystal Palace Park, Sydenham.

Of Paxton's public parks those at Liverpool and Birkenhead probably remain most nearly as Paxton intended.

There is nothing to see at Hyde Park, although the foundations of the Crystal Palace are said to be still beneath the turf. The site was on the large open area on the south side of the park between Rotten Row and the South Carriage Drive. There is a memorial to the Great Exhibition behind the Royal Albert Hall although this is a long way west of the site of the exhibition.

There is little now to see at Sydenham which has any connection with Paxton. Apart from the memorial only belts of trees, some rather forlorn steps and terraces and one of the lakes remains, although the latter retains the prehistoric monsters in replica. The palace itself perished in the greatest spectacle ever seen in that place of spectacles when it was burned down during the night of 30th November 1936. The National Recreation Centre now occupies the centre of the park and work on improving the remainder was in progress as this book went to press.

Mentmore in Buckinghamshire probably now retains more work by Paxton in one place than anywhere else but neither house nor park are open to the public.

Chatsworth, still the home of the Dukes of Devonshire, remains the place most evocative of Paxton. The house is usually open to the public during the afternoons from Wednesdays to Sundays from April to early October and the gardens are open daily during those months. Although the Great Conservatory and the Lily House are gone there remain Paxton's Conservative Wall, the rockworks and waterfalls and the Emperor Fountain. Paxton's house, Barbrook, was demolished a few years ago.

Across the park is the village of Edensor, largely designed by Paxton. At the top of the sloping churchyard are the tombs of the Dukes, including that of Paxton's friend and employer the sixth Duke. In the centre of the churchyard is the quite imposing tomb of Paxton and his wife.

BIBLIOGRAPHY

Two biographies of Joseph Paxton have been written:

Paxton and the Bachelor Duke; Violet Markham; Hodder and Stoughton, 1935.

The Works of Sir Joseph Paxton; G. F. Chadwick; Architectural Press, 1961.

These are largely complementary, the former being mainly concerned with Paxton's personal life and the latter with his work.

Most of the books on Chatsworth contain few references to Paxton but see the admirable booklet obtainable there:

The Garden at Chatsworth; Derbyshire Countryside Ltd., 1970.

Of the events of 1851 and the Crystal Palaces there is a large, and still growing, literature of which the following is a selection:

London 1851, The Year of the Great Exhibition; Eric de Maré; The Folio Society, 1972.

The Building Erected for the Great Exhibition in Hyde Park 1851; Charles Downes; 1852 (facsimile issued by the Victoria and Albert Museum, 1971).

The Crystal Palace: 1851 to 1936; Patrick Beaver; Hugh Evelyn, 1970.

The Great Exhibition: 1851; Yvonne ffrench; Harvill, 1950.

The Great Exhibition of 1851: A Commemorative Album; C. H. Gibbs-Smith; HMSO, 1950 and 1964.

The Phoenix Suburb; Alan Warwick; Blue Boar Press, 1972.